DISASTER WARNING!

TSUNAMIS

by Rex Ruby

Consultant: Beth Gambro
Reading Specialist, Yorkville, Illinois

Minneapolis, Minnesota

Teaching Tips

Before Reading

- Look at the cover of the book. Discuss the picture and the title.
- Ask readers to brainstorm a list of what they already know about tsunamis. What can they expect to see in the book?
- Go on a picture walk, looking through the pictures to discuss vocabulary and make predictions about the text.

During Reading

- Read for purpose. Encourage readers to think about the kinds of things that might happen during a tsunami.
- Ask readers to look for the details of the book. What are the dangers of a tsunami?
- If readers encounter an unknown word, ask them to look at the sounds in the word. Then, ask them to look at the rest of the page. Are there any clues to help them understand?

After Reading

- Encourage readers to pick a buddy and reread the book together.
- Ask readers to name two ways to stay safe during a tsunami. Find the pages that tell about these things.
- Ask readers to write or draw something they learned about tsunamis.

Credits

Cover and title page, © Mimadeo/iStock and © deepblue4you/iStock; 3, © John Blottman/iStock; 5, © Alex Izeman/Shutterstock; 7, © Dzmitry Melnikau/Shutterstock; 9, © Stock City/Shutterstock; 10–11, © Sach336699/Shutterstock; 13, © Steven Harrie/iStock; 14–15, © mTaira/Shutterstock; 17, Adansijav Official/Shutterstock; 19, © The World Traveller/iStock; 21, © SOPA Images Limited /Alamy Stock Photo; 22T, © muratart/Shutterstock; 22M, © Sipa USA/Alamy Stock Photo; 22B, © StevenDillon/iStock; 23TL, © Camera Kidd/Shutterstock; 23TM, © Tada Images/Shutterstock; 23TR, Beach Media/Shutterstock; 23BL, © richcarey/iStock; 23BR, Rod Haestier/Alamy Stock Photo.

See BearportPublishing.com for our statement on Generative AI Usage.

Library of Congress Cataloging-in-Publication Data

Names: Ruby, Rex author
Title: Tsunamis / by Rex Ruby.
Description: Minneapolis, Minnesota : Bearport Publishing Company, [2026] |
  Series: Disaster warning! | "Bearcub books." | Includes bibliographical
  references and index. | Audience term: juvenile
Identifiers: LCCN 2024062294 (print) | LCCN 2024062295 (ebook) | ISBN
  9798892329910 library binding | ISBN 9798895774229 paperback | ISBN
  9798895771082 ebook
Subjects: LCSH: Tsunamis--Juvenile literature
Classification: LCC GC221.5 .R83 2026 (print) | LCC GC221.5 (ebook) | DDC
  551.46/37--dc23/eng/20250221
LC record available at https://lccn.loc.gov/2024062294
LC ebook record available at https://lccn.loc.gov/2024062295

Copyright © 2026 Bearport Publishing Company. All rights reserved. No part of this publication may be reproduced in whole or in part, stored in any retrieval system, or transmitted in any form or by any means, electronic, mechanical, photocopying, recording, or otherwise, without written permission from the publisher. Bearport Publishing is a division of FlutterBee Education Group.

For more information, write to Bearport Publishing, 3500 American Blvd W, Suite 150, Bloomington, MN 55431.

Contents

A Wall of Water 4

Tsunami Facts 22

Glossary 23

Index 24

Read More 24

Learn More Online 24

About the Author 24

A Wall of Water

A loud roar comes from far away.

Soon, a huge wave races toward the beach.

Warning!

A **tsunami** is coming!

Say tsunami like tsoo-NAH-mee

The tall wave reaches the shore.

Crash!

It moves onto land.

The wave covers everything with water.

Most waves are caused by wind.

But tsunamis are different.

They are often caused by **earthquakes**.

An earthquake is when the ground shakes.

Sometimes, this happens below the ocean.

When the **seafloor** moves, a wave forms above.

As the wave moves toward shore, it gets bigger.

This wave is called a tsunami.

It moves very fast.

Zoom!

13

Tsunamis can cause **disasters**.

People can get hit by the waves.

Tsunamis can wipe away homes, too.

How can you tell a tsunami is coming?

Sometimes, you can feel the earthquake.

Just before a tsunami, water moves away from a beach.

To stay safe, get away from the sea.

Go to a high place.

This makes it harder for the water to reach you.

Tsunamis can last for hours.

Stay where it is safe and dry.

More waves might come your way!

Tsunami Facts

A tsunami can move as fast as a plane.

Hawaii is the state that is most likely to get a tsunami.

Tsunami is a Japanese word. It means **harbor** wave.

Glossary

disasters events that cause much damage or suffering

earthquakes sudden shaking of the ground

harbor an area of water near land where ships stay

seafloor the bottom of the ocean

tsunami a large wave or group of strong waves that come onto land

Index

beach 4, 16
earthquakes 8, 10, 16
land 6
ocean 10
seafloor 10
waves 4, 6, 8, 10, 14, 22
wind 8

Read More

Kerry, Isaac. *Tsunamis (Wild Earth Science).* North Mankato, MN: Pebble, 2022.

Murray, Julie. *Tsunamis (Natural Disasters).* Minneapolis: Abdo Zoom, 2025.

Learn More Online

1. Go to **FactSurfer.com** or scan the QR code below.
2. Enter "**Tsunamis Warning**" into the search box.
3. Click on the cover of this book to see a list of websites.

About the Author

Rex Ruby lives in Minnesota with his family. Going for a swim is one of his favorite things to do.